When Yestertime Was Now

Copyright © 2019-20 by Susan Lindsley, all rights reserved. No part of this book may be reproduced, stored or transmitted in any form or by electronic or mechanical means without expressed written permission from Susan Lindsley and/or ThomasMax Publishing. An exception is granted for the use of brief passages used for review purposes.

ISBN-13: 978-1-7334044-0-2
ISBN-10: 1-7334044-0-6

First Printing, March 2020

Published by:

ThomasMax Publishing
P.O. Box 250054
Atlanta, GA 30325

When Yestertime Was Now

Susan Lindsley

ThomasMax
Your Publisher
For The 21st Century

ACKNOWLEDGMENTS

The title poem, "When Yestertime Was Now" took first place in the Walt Whitman Poetry Contest sponsored by the Southeastern Writers Association in 2019.

"Memorial Day" (page 12) was published in *The Reach of Song*, The Georgia Poetry Society, 2018, page 99.

The photograph of the ghost riders (page 15) was taken by Richard Cranium and is used with his permission.

"The Golden Years" (page 22) was published in *The Reach of Song*, The Georgia Poetry Society, 2017, page 119.

The photograph of the mule deer doe reflected in the Powder River, Broadus, Montana (page 25) was published in *Possum Cops, Poachers and the Counterfeit Game Warden*, page 254.

The photograph of the child (Peter) (page 27) is used with the permission of his parents.

"The Unwritten Poem" (page 28) placed third in the Founders Awards and was published in *The Reach of Song*, The Georgia Poetry Society, 2018, page 24.

The Confederate army lieutenant (page 38) is the author's great-grandfather who was killed at the Battle of Cedar Creek. The picture is a copy of the photograph taken of him shortly before his death.

Peggy Mercer, Georgia Author of the Year, poet, and songwriter, helped me select poems for this collection, and I am also grateful to her for her enthusiastic endorsement of the book.

As always, my life partner Gail Cabisius has encouraged me and also helped select which poems would be included.

Thank you Lee Clevenger, Preston Ward and ThomasMax Publishing for your support and your belief in my works.

OTHER BOOKS BY SUSAN LINDSLEY

Novels, Southern historical
    The Bottom Rail*
    When Darkness Fell*

Memoirs
    Blue Jeans and Pantaloons in YESTERPLACE
    Possum Cops, Poachers and the Counterfeit Game Warden*

Biography
    Susan Myrick of Gone With the Wind
    The Lindsleys of Westover

Edited Collections of works by others
    Myrick Memories
    Margaret Mitchell: A Scarlett or a Melanie?*
    Luther Lindsley: His Literary Works

Poetry
    O Yesterplace and other poems (out of print)
    Christmas Gift

Short Story collections
    Emperor of the United American States (out of print)
    Whitetails and Tall Tales *
    Finding Bigfoot*

Specialty Book (Photography)
    Wildlife in Persimmon Paradise*

---

*Award winners

IN MEMORY OF

**JUNE ELAINE KITCHENS SMITH
PEABODY HIGH CLASS OF 1954**

WHOSE WRITINGS AND POETRY INSPIRED ME

TABLE OF CONTENTS

When Yestertime Was Now	1
Someone's Yesterplace	2
Old Yellow River	3
My Soul Is Seeking Silence	4
Spring of 1999	5
Musical Alpine Visions	6
The Swan	7
Flirtation	8
Musical Images	9
The Closed Door	10
Georgia	11
Memorial Day	12
Remembering June	13
Dooley Kitten	14
The Devil's Herd	15
The Crack of Dawn	16
One Thanksgiving Day	17
Autumn Leaves	18
As I Lie Dying	19
The Buzzard	20
Remembering Yesterplace	21
The Golden Years	22
Visions at Symphony	23
Dawn	24
The Morning after Your Death	25
The Night Wind's Song	26
Paths	27
The Unwritten Poem	28
Music in the Air	29
Yesterplace Is Calling Me	30
Last October	31
Write Me a Story	32
Morning	33
The Woods Where I Was Young	34
Choices	35
The Bliss of Solitude	36
Spring Morning	37
Spirit of the Old South	38
I Fell to Yesterday	39
Music of the Evening	40
Make a Rainbow	41
If I Could Only Sing	42
Rocky Snow	43

Stardust	44
Where Yesterplace Once Was	45
The Joys of Camping	46
A Sheet of Paper	47
Remembering Dolly	48
Grandma's Pastel Lace	49
The Sheriff	50

WHEN YESTERTIME WAS NOW

The land is empty now of corn and cattle, and the fields are growing houses in the sun
Where in my years of childhood I was free to follow where the creeks and shadows run.

But still, I smell the dusty dry aroma of the summer hay
Where I would lie at night to watch the stars that shot across the Milky Way.

Oh, many are the sights and sounds of yestertime I never can forget
But hold forever in my mind. The hot and heavy scent of leather and of sweat,
The clanking jingle of the harness and the chewing sound
       of horse's teeth on winter hay,
The swinging lanterns on a possum hunt and Spot's distinctive bay
That rang against the hills and filled an autumn night
When autumn Hunter's Moon spread its golden light
Upon an early snow.

And now, no matter where I go
I disremember lands that grow a crop of houses down the street
But see my yesterplace
And horses
And moonlight on the hayfields smelling sweet.

SOMEONE'S YESTERPLACE

The house is dying
In the grip of oaks and elms
And miles of kudzu vine.

Tracks where mice have ventured
Mark forty years of dust
On floors of polished-pine.

Wrens now sing their welcomes
To the rising sun
From perches on the cabinets
Where they've nested
Since children filled with mischief
Broke the windows just for fun.

But left behind
Forgotten daffodils
Still blossom in the shade
And yellow roses climb the trees
To reach for sun
And cast their sweet perfume
Into the July air.

A rotting rope still dangles
Where the children
Long ago,
Swung themselves
And laughter
Through their summer days
And longed to reach the sky.

A wash pot rusts beside the spring
Where now the crawfish
And the bullfrogs reign.

No one comes from yesterday
And no one from tomorrow
To look or to remember
The lives, the loves, the laughter
Or the tears
That once echoed
In this yesterplace.

THE OLD YELLOW RIVER

The old Yellow River sings a song
She sings of the lovers in the days of long ago
She sings of the twilight's afterglow.

The old Yellow River sings a song
She sings of the dreamers and the dreams the dreamers dream
She sings of the mysteries in the stream.

The old Yellow River sings a song
She sings of remembrance and its echoes in the breeze
She sings of the deepest winter freeze.

The old Yellow River sings a song
She sings of the moonlight and romance of long ago,
She sings of the deepest love I know.

The old Yellow River sings a song
She sings of my sorrow deeper than the deepest sea,
She sings of my love she took from me.

MY SOUL IS SEEKING SILENCE

My soul is seeking silence
And the stillness
Of the marsh that lies
Beside the sea
Where the only sound that seeps into the soul
Is the rolling of the tide
That beats within the heart that beats in me.

My soul is seeking silence,
All the vast and empty silence
Of the snow on winter nights
When nothing but the whisper of the snow
Upon the cedar
Breaks the silent solitude of night.

My soul is seeking silence,
Where the scarlet leaves of autumn
Whisper like a ripple in the river,
Where the sunlight sings a silent song
And waltzes like a dream upon the autumn air.

My soul is seeking silence,
Where the silent sands
Are rolling to forever like the sea
And the humming of the wind upon the sand
Is but the silent humming and the pulsing
Of the blood that sings in me.

My soul is seeking silence
But the only sound of silence
Is the distant, far away
Within my dreams.

SPRING OF 1999

Children running with the wind and tossing kites on high,
Robins throwing songs of love into the April sky,

Shadows and the sunlight in a wild erotic dance,
Flowers rioting color over meadows' wide expanse,

Breezes blowing coolness in the warming morning air,
Dogwoods bowing in the wind like priestesses at prayer,

Pastel greens upon the trees and running up the vines,
Songs that seep into the soul with music from the pines,

Spring erupting everywhere and perfume on the breeze,
Springtime blossoms everywhere, but pollen makes me sneeze.

MUSICAL ALPINE VISIONS

The day begins to stir awake, for sleeping now is done,
And Dawn is slipping westward, calling softly to the sun

Lighting up the mountain like a stallion tall and proud
To throw a coat of silver on the rising thundercloud.

Rivers catch the sunlight with a shudder and a roar
Sliding morning sunlight with them to the valley floor.

On the mountain, glaciers gleaming cold and icy blue
Weep until the evening sends the twilight shadows through.

Somewhere over mountains in the endless mountain skies
Thunder always tumbles where the angry lightning flies.

Whispers from the mountain when the wind begins to rise
Echo lonely music in the lonely endless skies.

Long before the twilight comes to kiss the mountain snow
Flowers of the summer bloom a day before they go.

Night comes to the mountain, lays her head upon its breast
And slumbers in the valley like a lover home to rest.

The power of the mountains and the power of the sun
Roll on to forever after human life is done.

THE SWAN

I saw a purple swan upon a mirror of the sky
Who sang to me of hope and love as she went floating by

Rising with the morning mist the magic of her singing
Echoed softly in the air like bells of crystal ringing

Gliding on the mirror, making ripples in the sky,
She saw what I was thinking with her magic crystal eye

She called to me to step into her mirror of the sky
And glide into forever on her lover's lullaby

So there beside tomorrow in the mirror of the dawn
I rode into forever in the music of the swan.

FLIRTATION

The golden maple spread her skirt
Before the flirting breeze
To show her courting lover
All the glory of her leaves.

But overcome with shyness
She just whispered to the breeze
Who gently stroked her naked limbs
And kissed her golden leaves.

MUSICAL IMAGES

Music like a sailing ship upon a magic sea
Takes me down the river with a thousand sights to see

Butterflies with amber wings above a silver stream
Knights and dancing ladies from a storybook or dream

Starlight drifting softly like the yellow leaves of fall
Ladies in their satin laces going to a ball

Swallows swirling through the air like shadows of the night
Blue and red and purple streamers on a yellow kite

Oceans calling softly to the shadows on the shore
Rocking horses rocking in the window at the store

Horses on a carousel or prancing in a show
Redbirds on a cedar hanging heavy from the snow

Children full of laughter and with cotton-candy faces
Memories of my yestertimes and of my yesterplaces.

THE CLOSED DOOR

Oh, would that I could be as free as when I was a child
When all that ever crossed my mind was running free and wild,

Running with the sunrise as it tumbled down the hill,
Taking summer showers in the falls beside the mill,

Jumping semi-naked in the mud down in the sty,
Always asking someone simple questions starting, "Why...?"

Racing over hayfields with the shooting stars at night,
Chasing after fireflies with their magic flashing light.

Oh, would that I could be so free, in yesterplace once more,
But we cannot return to where the years have closed the door.

GEORGIA

Have you seen a bluebird with the sun upon its breast,
Or laid beside a campfire in the twilight for your rest?

Have you heard a gobbler calling all the world awake,
Or lived a mallard morning by a misty mountain lake?

Have you heard the timber doodle sing his courting flights,
Or seen the rising moon a flaming red on autumn nights?

Have you smelled the forests or the fields of new-mown hay,
Or waded salty marshes where the river meets the bay?

Have you seen the 'possums feasting in persimmon trees
Or smelled the wine of muscadines upon the autumn breeze?

Have you seen the dogwood shading springtime daffodils,
Or seen the wild azaleas blazing orange on the hills?

Have you rocked upon the porch at twilight every day,
Or smelled magnolia blossoms from your window every May?

Have you seen an antlered buck in shadows, slipping by,
Or watched the red tail circle lazy circles in the sky?

Come make your home in Georgia, plant your roots into her sod,
Where mountain, sea and valley all have felt the kiss of God.

MEMORIAL DAY

I hear the sound of drumming and the sound of marching feet
As memories of our yesterdays and living soldiers meet.

Uniforms are stiff as starch and every leg is creased,
And Taps is bringing tears as we remember our deceased.

Soldiers march forever on, in pride, to honor gain
In the burning deserts or the jungle's steaming rain.

But all I see are memories marching in the twilight mist
And bodies on the battlefield that glory never kissed.

Honorable Mention, Smith Mosely Award, Southeastern Writers Association, 2010
Reach of Song, Georgia Poetry Society, 2018

REMEMBERING JUNE

They called last night
To tell me you had died.
But with the morning mail
You came alive again.

You wrote of things you never spoke before—
Of children and your grands
I never knew,
As if to keep alive
Yourself
Within my heart.

But I could not forget
In all the years I may have left
The friendship of our youth,
The laughter that you brought
Into my life—
The joy of finding you again
When fifty years had passed.

The rhymes and words you shared
Are with me still
And led me to a lifetime
With a pen
And love of empty pages
Waiting to be filled.

June Kitchens (Smith) was the author's best friend in high school. June wrote rhymed poetry with tight rhythm and inspired this author to continue to write.

DOOLEY KITTEN

Dooley kitten, nearly white,
Shadow prowler of the night,
With your yellow tiger eyes,
Fur like summer cotton skies,

In a game you like to play
You're a tiger stalking prey,
Flying like a bird with wings,
Making snakes from vines and things,

Dooley kitten—what a cat!
Stealing feathers from my hat,
On the prowl from room to room,
Stalking dustpans and the broom,

Batting things around the house
Clawing on the company couch.
Pulling on my knitting thread,
Prowling when I go to bed.

Toilet paper everywhere,
Through the den, across the chair.
You think my everything's a toy
Simply made to bring you joy,

Stalking tiger, bird in flight,
Prowler of the shadowed night,
You're my heart! What joy you bring!
Though you tear up everything.

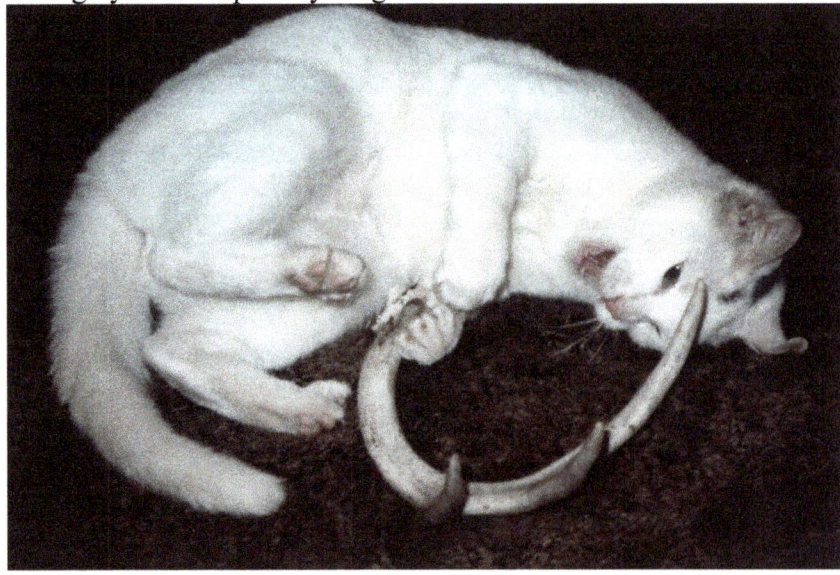

THE DEVIL'S HERD

I heard the thunder rumble as the cattle galloped by
And lightning from the hoof beats flashed across the cloudy sky.

They ran along a canyon down a rough and winding trail
And right behind the thunder came the cowboys' mournful wail.

But always just behind the herd, too far to throw a rope,
They ride into forever and they never have a hope

Of rounding up the Devil's herd that's running wild and free.
So when it thunders at the dawn, look up and you will see

The cattle black and shining, striking lightning in the sky
And fear in living cowboys of the Devil when they die.
_____
May be sung to the music of "Ghost Riders in the Sky."

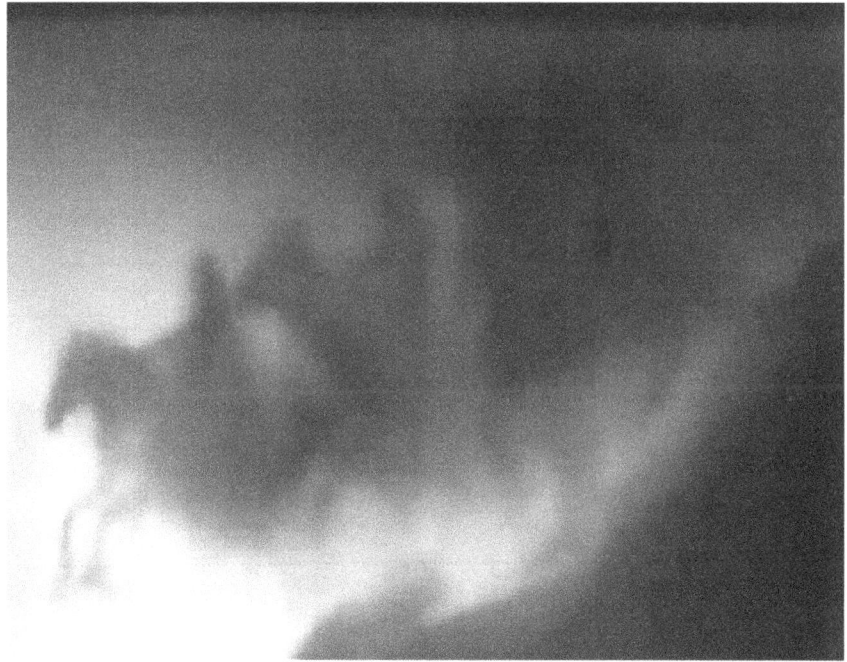

THE CRACK OF DAWN

I heard the crack of dawn and know that's why I came awake,
For every dawn I hear the noise of day about to break.

Every day I rush about, afraid that night will fall
For if it does and breaks apart, can it be fixed at all?

Or like a broken egg will night just spill out every where
To mingle with the broken dawn and then be lost somewhere?

Heaven help us if the dawn and night become a jumble
Because the evening then would crack and dawn would take the tumble.

ONE THANKSGIVING DAY

The winter morning coming
Puts the stars to flight
And the early morning breeze,
Tickling all the trees,
Giggles with delight.

The winter's bitter freeze
Frosts the world with white,
And the morning mist,
Sun-kissed,
Shivers with delight.

My heart goes to the meadow
With the fawns at early light,
Finding pleasure
Without measure,
Romping with delight.

AUTUMN LEAVES

The dancing leaves have put a song into my feet
So with the autumn breezes I am dancing down the street

I dance with autumn sunlight of a golden autumn hue
And fly with autumn breezes where no other ever flew.

I'll hold the gold and scarlet leaves forever to my breast
Nestled like my lover in an afternoon of rest

I'll laugh with all the maple trees, those red and flaming flirts,
Dropping leaves as slowly as a stripper drops her skirts.

Before the winter takes the leaves onto the forest floor,
I'll store the autumn in my heart beyond forevermore.

AS I LIE DYING

The battle ended
And the living fled.
Around me lay ten thousand dead
And silence,
A quiet so deep
I heard my shadow breathe.
Hawks and eagles
And the vultures came,
Silent circles on the thermals
Waiting,
Sailing overhead,
Like some children's toys
Upon a string
As clouds encroached.
Silent as the battlefield
Ice fell.
I heard the crystals shatter
As they clashed into each other.
Somewhere in the silence
Of the carrion
A whispered plea
Arose and grated in the air
"Mama."
The voice my own.
And silence fell.

THE BUZZARD

Lying in the meadow, watching clouds go drifting by
I saw a buzzard catch the wind and circle in the sky.

What wonders could that buzzard see while circling far away?
Could he see the river where it spreads into the bay?

Could he see across the hill
Where the soldiers daily drill?

Would he notice trees at all,
Or their difference, spring and fall?

Could he see where children meet
Playing hopscotch in the street?

Could he see the railroad track,
Twisting, curving, turning back,
Laid by slaves so long ago,
Twisting, so the train goes slow?

Has he ever thought to kill
To get himself another meal?

Or does he circle in the skies
Using nose and never eyes,
Always sniffing for a stink?
—Can a buzzard even think?

As he circled far away,
Did he see me where I lay?

Would he think me simply chow,
Dead as any horse or cow?

Thinking of the buzzard, I soon fell into a doze,
And when I woke
(And it's no joke)
There he stood
With bloody hood,
And in his beak, my nose.

REMEMBERING YESTERPLACE

It's a time we all remember for the beauty and the grace
Of the columned mansions on the hills of yesterplace.

We remember dogwoods and the jasmine on the hill
The sound of banjos plunking when the night is deep and still.

We remember banners flying, and all the ladies fair,
The tall and gallant soldiers, and the trumpets mighty blare.

We still remember cotton and the wealth it used to bring,
We even sing the songs of hope the slaves themselves would sing.

We choose to disremember all the sadness and disgrace
Of the days of slavery when we think of yesterplace.

Gates to Georgia's antebellum capitol building

THE GOLDEN YEARS

I've plastic in my eyeballs and a speaker in my ear,
A plastic bag and tubing substituting for my rear,

I've plastic in my vessels and have metal in my knee.
A pump to time my heartbeat and tri-focals just to see.

I've glue to hold my uppers and a rod along my spine
A wig to hide my baldness and some pills before I dine.

They say these are our golden years to give them more appeal,
But they are no more golden than my hip of stainless steel.
_____
Reach of Song, Georgia Poetry Society, 2017, p. 119

VISIONS AT SYMPHONY

Ships that fill their sails with wind and plow the stormy seas,
Scarlet leaves that leap and dance upon the autumn breeze.

Ponies on a carousal with painted wooden side
Waiting for the children with a mighty charger's pride.

Acrobats who toss themselves across the empty air,
Snowy mountains people climb because the peaks are there.

Mountain-meadow flowers blooming in the summer snow,
Stallions charging over fields where summer grasses grow.

Soldiers marching briskly to the war that lies ahead,
Flowers dancing in the sun, yellow, pink and red.

Foals that wobble at the dawn and leap with fading light,
Hunter's moon that lays a golden aura on the night.

Lovers in the shadows by the river, holding hands,
Laughing children building pirate castles in the sands.

Music, like a lily, opens in the winter air
Pouring out the pictures it collects from everywhere.

DAWN

Dawn
The ocean pulls at fog
To hide her face
As I would hide my soul.
I weep.

The shell
The sea has tossed
Against my foot
Is twin to one at home
The ocean graced us with
While we strolled these very sands
Beneath the July sun.

Sunlight flares
Against a yellow kite
As children's laughter
Shatters silence
Like broken glass.

The fog retreats
Before the rising wind
That brings the smell of you—
Of menthol cigarettes—
From someone walking down the shore.

I turn away
From laughter, joy and sun,
And the final promise
You could not keep
"I will be safely home,"
The last you spoke when leaving for Iraq.

_____
October 20, 2006, class work at South Carolina Writers
Conference, teacher, Kwame Dawes.

THE MORNING AFTER YOUR DEATH

Morning dawns
And Lonely, like a mist,
Rises from the pond to seize my soul.

Birds fling morning love songs to the air,
A heron, black against the sky,
Drops honking in, to perch upon an ancient oak
Whose heavy tears are bleeding to the earth.
A gobbler calls and struts before the hens with hope and love—
His challenge to the dawn to sling the sun across the sky.

The pond erupts as one lone bass goes dancing for the day.
Silence falls, a moment only,
A single whip-o-wailing rips into my heart.

You would have loved this day!
The challenge of the bass,
The gobbler strutting spring away,
The smaller birds all nesting yet again,
The dew-wet web a spider spun last night
Would make you smile with joy—
A perfect dawn if but a deer,
A buck, a doe or fawn,
Would step forth from the mists,
Reflect into the mirror for a drink.

God knows it's dead I'd rather be than alive to see this day!
When they play taps for you at twilight,
I'll be there.

THE NIGHT WIND'S SONG

I hear the call of yesterplace upon the night wind's song
Calling like a lover to come home where I belong

All the songs that yesterplace is sending on the wind
Echo childhood music that I long to hear again

For I can hear the laughter when the night wind starts to blow
Coming from the people of my childhood long ago

On the night winds I can smell the smell of dirt and rain,
And the smell of horse's sweat and summertime again.

The night wind brings again the song of raindrops on the tin
In my mind I hear the fireplace crackle once again.

Oh, Night Wind, I must heed your call and leave the city's race
And turn my footsteps homeward with the dawn to yesterplace.

PATHS

I saw a picture made of me way back in Yesterplace
Before these sixty years had walked their paths across my face.

I wear the path to sorrow for a love lost long ago,
And chasms where the tears of joy and those of sadness flow.

The trails of laughter seem to stretch beside my eyes for miles,
And roadways run around my lips from laughter and from smiles.

The ditches in between my eyes from years of asking why
Are topped by furrows from a life of gazing at the sky.

Our childhood is a face of neither sadness nor of smiles,
But waits for laughter and the tears to map the many miles.

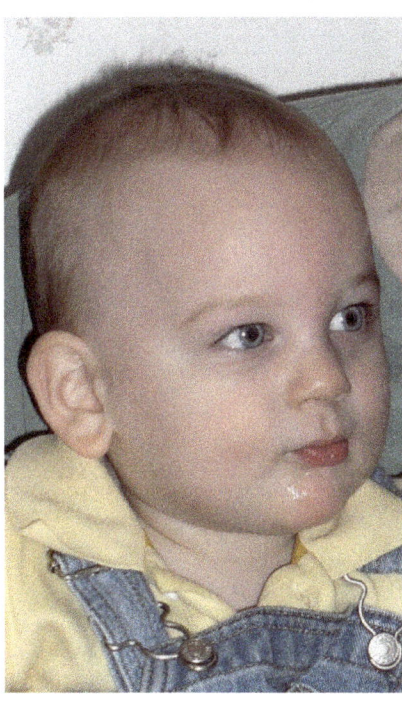

THE UNWRITTEN POEM

I dreamed a poem
But when I took my pen
In hand
The words
Like ping-pong balls
Tumbled from the table
To the floor
Where my kitty
Batted them around
And rolled them
From my thoughts
And out the door.

Third Place, Georgia Poetry Society Founders Award, Fall 2017
Honorable Mention, Writers-Editors Network Poetry Contest, 2017

MUSIC IN THE AIR
  At Symphony

I let my soul go flowing with the music in the air,
Marching with the marchers with a military flair,

Floating like a lazy leaf when violins are soft,
Until the horns and bugles rise to carry me aloft.

With the drummers drumming I see children marching by,
Eager for the battle where the old and children die.

I can hear the cannon and its never-ending roar,
I can see the soldiers march like lemmings to the shore.

Softly falls the music like a mother's lullaby
Or waltzes for a rainbow should it waltz across the sky,

Music for the moonlight throwing shadows on the snow.
But soldiers hear the drumming, and to war the soldiers go,

Marching to the tempo of the trumpet's mighty blare
Till the sound of cannon and the dying fill the air.

Losing now, the soldiers filled with terror and with dread
Flee and leave behind them all their mangled and their dead.

When the trumpets rise again and music starts to soar
Fleeing soldiers turn around to face the cannon's roar.

Again the drummers drumming call the children out to fight
And I can only wonder: In a war is there a right?

Strings begin to whisper like some distant ocean shore
But the brass is rising with the booming cannon's roar.

With the sound of victory when the dying's finally done
Comes wailing of the mothers who have lost their every son.

The sounds of peace are flowing with the music in the air,
The living can go home again if any home is there.

Shostakovich: Symphony No. 7 in C Major, Op.60, "Leningrad" (1941)

YESTERPLACE IS CALLING ME

Yesterplace is calling me like voices from the grave,
Voices of the children and the heroes and the brave,

Whispers from the dreamers who would dare to go alone,
Music from the yesterplaces many years now gone.

I can hear the voices when the night wind starts to blow,
Calling me as softly as a whisper in the snow—

All my yesterpeople calling me to yesterplace
Over many centuries and a thousand miles of space.

I can see the soldiers in their butternut and gray
Who took a Minnie ball and lived to talk about the day.

I can hear the bugler calling children out to fight
And the drummer drumming and the marching in the night.

I can hear the wagons and the cracking of the whips,
People walking westward by their rolling prairie ships.

I can hear the horses but the sounds are growing faint
Cowboys ride on wheels today for no one wants Old Paint.

I can hear the drying winds across the middle land
Rolling down the furrows turning all the air to sand.

I can hear the native and his loud defiant cry
Pushed onto the desert to ensure his people die.

I can hear from far away a rising call to arms
Spreading from the city to the villages and farms.

I can hear the muskets on that distant April day
Turning thoughts of freedom to the ancient Roman way.

I can hear the screaming where the Pilgrim leaders dwell,
Where they used the name of Christ to create earthly hell.

All my yesterpeople call me back to yesterplace
Over all the centuries and a thousand miles of space.

LAST OCTOBER

A bleakness creeps into my soul as Lonely settles in
Each time I face the darkness and the missing you again.

I'd like to see the fires of winter burning down to coals
While we talk throughout the night and share our very souls.

I'd like to help you dress again your house and Christmas tree
And pick some flowers with you, and vacation by the sea.

I'd like to walk the trails with you, and fish the rushing streams
And have you fill my living as you always fill my dreams.

But Lonely won't be run away, though goodness knows I've tried—
It's pumped within my heart since last October when you died.

WRITE ME A STORY

Write me some poetry or sing me a song,
Tell me adventures of monsters and slime.

Put me a shiver down deep in my bones
Play me some music with mystical tones.

Tell me that dinosaurs really can fly
Convince me the moon is an alien's eye.

Write me a story of stallions that dance,
And sing about lovers and perfect romance.

Write me a song that's always in tune
Of childhood and horses and fishing in June.

Tell me of horses that rumble the sky
And stories of battles and children who fly.

Tell me the sagas of pirates at sea—
The pirates of childhood I wanted to be.

Tell me of fairies too tiny to see
Who ride on the back of a wasp or a bee.

Give me the visions and magic you speak—
A life full of stories is all that I seek.

Honorable Mention, Smith Mosely Poetry Award,
Southeastern Writers Workshop, 2007

MORNING

The sky is dark and dreary
And the stars are hanging weary,
Hanging weary in the sky,

Tiny lanterns on the ceiling
All the stars are slowly reeling,
Slowly reeling through the sky;

All the northern lights go prancing
Like a pagan woman dancing
And romancing in the sky;

The weary sun a-borning
Finds a cold and dreary morning,
Cold and dreary like the sky;

The sun is climbing higher,
Climbing higher, spring is nigher,
Climbing higher in the sky.

All the dreary world was thirsting
For the spring that now is bursting
Now is bursting from the sky;

A bluebird soon is singing,
Singing till his joy is ringing,
Ringing from the morning sky.

THE WOODS WHERE I WAS YOUNG

How many are the years since last I strolled into this wood,
Since last I stood
Beside this mighty oak that then
Was but a sapling, and the fen
That lies below the hill was shelter for so many things—
For geese on lengthy flights to rest their wings,
For deer to find a refuge from the hunter's autumn stalk,
For grouse to drum upon a log, and quail to talk
With merry whistle as the evening turns to night.
A place that turns to ghostly shadows when the evening light
Has fallen into dark, where evening breezes sway
The honeysuckle vine that in the dark looks like a nun who kneels to pray.

Oh, how I've missed this wood, with trees in winter standing tall and bare,
With Easter lilies scattered through the shadows by the spring, where wild azaleas flare
Their colors pink and orange by the creek, where I would swim until the autumn chill
Would chase me from the swimming hole below the mill.

The heavy tread of people and the many years have torn the woods apart
And left me only sadness and the memories clutched within my heart.

CHOICES

The mockingbird loves music more than flowers of the spring,
So now he sings the songs that all the other birds can sing.

The meadow lark is also marked by something he likes best—
The lines of fences zagging through the golden fields out west.

Because he feels a little shame in seeking just the dead,
The buzzard floats forever with his face a blushing red.

Eagles saw the mountains standing tall against the sky
And thought that over mountains was the perfect place to fly.

You can spend your lifetime singing like the mockingbirds,
So everything you say just echoes someone else's words.

You can sit on fences, never going anywhere,
Or you can be like buzzards and can scavenge everywhere.

Or you can build a nest upon a rainbow in the sky
And sail the music in your heart to soar where eagles fly.

Second Place, Distilled Experience Poetry Award,
Southeastern Writers Workshop, 2008

THE BLISS OF SOLITUDE

What a bliss is solitude, with silence everywhere,
When the only sound I hear is wind upon the air.

Silence of the woodlands when the snow is on the ground
Or a robin singing is the only woodland sound.

Silence of a morning when the mist begins to rise
Silence of the eagles when they circle in the skies

Silence of the twilight when the stars begin to glow
And somewhere in the far away the homing cattle low.

Silence of the river where it flows across the ground
Where an egret's footsteps are the only river sound.

Oh, the bliss of silence where no people will intrude—
Just the sound of silence and the bliss of solitude.

SPRING MORNING

Bluebirds in the sunlight when the morning comes in spring
Sunlight glowing softly on a flying mallard's wing

Children tripping gaily in the fallen autumn leaves
Whispers of the winter blowing cold upon the breeze

Silent morning stretching like a cat into the dawn
Roses running rampant now the daffodils are gone

Silver on the surface of the lake below the mist
Silver on the spider web the rising sun has kissed

Spring is bursting open with its promise for tomorrow
Joy and hope and love enough for everyone to borrow

Join the morning chorus, throw your soul into the skies
And fly into forever where the morning always flies.
_____

Inspired by Stravinsky:
Symphony in three movements (1945)

SPIRIT OF THE OLD SOUTH

The chimney stands alone beside by the well and battered pail
And paint has faded into gray that said "this house for sale."

The apple tree is choking under honeysuckle vine
Competing with a hundred years of running muscadine.

Magnolia limbs are heavy and the fence has gone to rust
But the open pathway shows new footprints in the dust.

A flower lies upon the stone that time has turned to gray
But still the words are showing: "Unknown Soldier, C. S. A."

Honorable Mention in the Julie L. Cannon "Spirit of the South" Contest, Southeastern Writers Workshop, June 2013

I FELL TO YESTERDAY

I leaned against a mirror and I fell to yesterday
Where I became a child again and all I did was play;

I watched a night of shooting stars while lying on the hay
That we had raked in windrows running every which-a-way;

I found a jumping rope and jumped a hundred-one hot peas
Then tied the rope onto a limb and made it my trapeze;

I watched some clouds go floating in a river at my feet
As they became the galleons of a pirate's raiding fleet.

I watched a summer shower running down a dusty road,
And underneath a rotting board I found myself a toad.

I jumped into a river but I landed in today
And in my pocket was the toad I brought from yesterday.

MUSIC OF THE EVENING

Though the twilight's hushed and still
Music echoes from the hill.

A hunting owl goes sailing by
A silent shadow in the sky.

A grunting buck pursues a doe
But again she snorts a "No."

A whip-poor-will calls sorrow out
Distant children yell and shout.

Secrets float upon the breeze,
Whispered by a thousand leaves.

A lightning bug flicks on his light
While songs caress the falling night.

MAKE A RAINBOW

When you're sad and dreary and the tears fill up your eyes
It's up to you if sorrow lives or if your sorrow dies.

Stir a bit of morning in the twilight purple sky,
Mix a summer shower with a wild coyote's cry.

Mix a bit of yesterday into your next tomorrow,
Stir up your nostalgia in your vat of pain and sorrow.

Mix up summer thunderheads with daffodils of spring,
Stir some falling snowflakes in the songs the robins sing.

Stir up all your laughter with the sparkle in your eyes
And you will make a rainbow in your cloudy summer skies.

IF I COULD ONLY SING

If I could only sing a song, I'd sing a song for you,
And if I were an artist, I'd not color skies with blue
But color them with laughter. I'd use flowers for the stars
And paint the ocean chocolate and make rocks from candy bars

On every storm of winter I would paint a golden glow
And all the trees of autumn I would drape with veils of snow
I'd write a song of magic and the notes would be the leaves
So I could throw my song of love upon the autumn breeze.

If the winter winds should come with ice and sleet and snow
They'd take my song of love with them where ever they should blow
When the flowers bloom again and winter turns to spring
My song of love would be the song you hear the blue bird sing

If I could only sing a song, I'd sing a song for you
For songs of you will fill my soul until forever's through.

ROCKY SNOW

He was just a saddle tramp who drifted on the plains
He rode through summer dust and the coldest winter rains.

Another drifter told him of a spotted mustang mare
Faster than the stallion winning races at the fair.

She was running wild and free across the mountains high
When the cowboy saw her, and her beauty made him cry
For she was running over hills like shadows over snow
Like a horse of childhood dreams the cowboy used to know.

So he gave a whistle, then another, loud and shrill
That flowed along behind her as she galloped down the hill.
Every day the cowboy rode out to the mountain side
As faithful with his whistle as the sun and moon and tide.

Soon she simply looked at him and waited for his call
Then snorted as she pranced away, her tail a waterfall.
When he offered her some feed and whistled her a tune
And waited in the shadows through the summer afternoon

She came prancing to the food just like the Denton mare.
Sunlight sparkled diamonds where the sun caressed her hair.
He rode her in the races with the name of Rocky Snow
And when he won himself a ranch, he tried to let her go.

He watched her cross the valley and go up the distant hill
But when he whistled his good bye, a whistle loud and shrill,
On the hill old Rocky seemed to search the distant haze
Then galloped to the barnyard where she's living out her days.

But cowboys on the Rocking S don't often see Old Snow,
For she is like the shadows, ever free to come and go.

___

The Denton Mare, Jenny, was supposed to be the daughter of Steeldust (or Steel Dust), who in turn was believed to be a founding sire of the Quarter Horse breed. Jenny received the nickname The Denton Mare after she began winning races in the town of Denton. She was owned at the time by Sam Bass, who later became an outlaw.

STARDUST

I threw my kite into the air, across the summer sky
And flew with it into the wind, where only eagles fly.

I flew above the rocky coast, above the sandy beach,
To the far horizon where forever cannot reach.

Later in the evening, where the night pursues the day,
I flew beyond the moonlight and the distant Milky Way.

When the morning sun came up, I finally drifted down
And left a trail of stardust on the snow and on the ground.

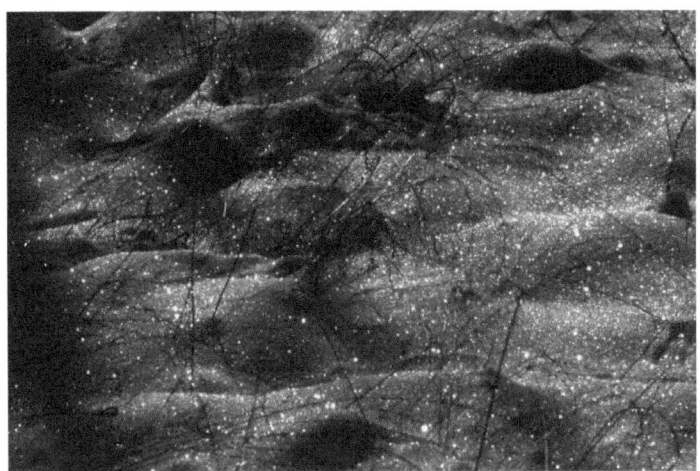

WHERE YESTERPLACE ONCE WAS

The land is growing houses just as far as I can see—
All across the meadows where the cattle used to be,

Over all the rolling fields that once were cotton-white,
Where the only sounds you heard were whippoorwills at night.

Now the squeals and screams of all the children running free
Fill the air of summer where the bobwhite used to be.

Sounds of Motorolas and of Sonys fill the air
So the deer and turkey now have gone away somewhere.

Oh, to go back home to where the fox and bunnies play,
Where the mockingbird makes magic music every day.

Oh, to smell again the earth that's rolled up in the spring
To taste again the peaches only Georgia summers bring.

Oh, to live again where rows of corn are growing tall
Where I saw the deer on misty mornings in the fall.

Oh, to hear the rocker squeaking on the porch again—
But all I have is city life and dreaming of back then.

THE JOYS OF CAMPING
      OR
ARE WE HAVING FUN YET?

Another midnight in a tent, I'm sleeping on the ground,
Hearing strangers snoring and some critters creeping round.

When the privy calls me long before the morning light
Through the pounding rain I go in deepest blackest night.

I sleep upon a bed of rocks, inside a zippered sack
So nothing I can ever do will ever ease my back.

When I wake at dawning, every joint a gripping pain,
I wonder if I'll ever even stand up straight again.

Buoys clanging through the night and wind up to a roar,
Visits by a skunk at dawn, and then it rains some more.

Children yelling all around and johnnie doors go *slam*.
Morning brings the smell of perking coffee, toast and jam.

So I get up hungry long before the sun is up,
But I can't light the Coleman, so no coffee for my cup.

Forget about a shower, for the water's never hot,
And anyhow, a faucet in a field is all I've got.

Every campground everywhere has somewhere got a *b'ar*,
So every night I load my stuff right back into the car.

Every time I pack my tent and gather up my togs
It isn't raining only rain, it's raining toads and frogs.

Oh, camping can be wholesome but I'll take a dollar bet
That others also ask if all the fun has started yet.

A SHEET OF PAPER

I am empty and alone.
I need your thoughts,
Your words and dreams,
Your memories of the mountains
And the sea.

Your dreams of what would be
Or might have been.

I need your songs of love,
Of paradise
And hell.

Your tales of horses and of cats,
Of honor and of reason.

Your dreams of worlds unknown
Beyond your time and space.

So lift your pen
And fill me with the joys
That lift your soul,
The pains that darken night,
The fears that haunt your dreams.

I welcome all your words.

REMEMBERING DOLLY

In summer we would run
Into the wind
Your back a slippery slope
Of sweat
That caked my naked legs
With salt.

In winter
You would wear a coat
As soft as rabbit fur
And I would lie along your back
My face upon your neck
To breathe your smell.

You gave me love and patience
Through the years
In all the games I played,
At mounting like Roy Rogers,
Or leaping over canyons
Great and small,
Or hanging by my heel and hand
To be an Indian on attack.
What torment you endured.

On that freezing fateful winter day
As you lay dying
I had to face
That final, fatal, cowboy deed.

GRANDMA'S PASTEL LACE

Spring is turning all the trees into a pastel lace
That brings to mind the curtains Grandma made when yesterplace
Was home, when everything within the house was made by hand
And Grandpa only had a single mule to help him work the land.

But I always loved to ride with him up on the rake to gather up the hay
In windrows that he later piled in shocks against a rainy day.

I well remember feeling I was such a fool
The first time Grandpa sent me out alone to hitch the mule
Up to the wagon for us all to go to town.
I forgot the trace chains, and the wagon shafts just fell onto the ground
When Gracie took a step and left the wagon standing there.

Oh, what wonder were aromas in the air
When Grandma fried up chicken and made her biscuits and her cake
For us to have an evening picnic and go fishing at the lake
Where all we ever caught would be a perch or two.
Anytime we caught too few
To bother taking home, Grandma showed us how to cook them in a special way,
To pack them in a coat of Georgia clay
And lay them in the coals as soon as flames were dying down.
When the clay was cracking, dry and brown,
We'd take them from the coals and let them cool, then peel the fish
And eat them with our hands—we never bothered with a fork or dish.

What memories has the morning stirred of yesterplace,
A time when life was harder, but the curtains were of lace.

THE SHERIFF

The boy upon the rocking horse was riding fast and hard
Chasing rustlers through the hills while rocking in his yard

Through the desert valleys with the rolling tumbleweed
Rode the gallant sheriff on a mighty silver steed

Up the rising mountains, down the canyons deep and wide
Dodging flying bullets when the rustlers turned and fired

Running down the hollows where the rushing rivers flow
Up across the ridges through the crunching ice and snow.

Soon the sheriff rode alone, the posse far behind,
While the fleeing rustlers ran across the sheriff's mind.

On and on the sheriff rode, a lawman must not fail—
But Mother's "Supper's ready" calls the lawman off the trail.

www.ingramcontent.com/pod-product-compliance
Lightning Source LLC
Chambersburg PA
CBHW060856090426
42736CB00025B/3495